Horizon Of Freedom

A force created a long time ago is ready to reunite.

Characterized by green or blue eyes surrounded by a dark color, they are an Elite Force.

In a remote planet of the galaxy the reunion is imminent as the conditions had been created.

Fer returns to the planet to locate and awaken these extraordinary beings.

Another adventure is ready for starting.

Are you part of this group?

This is an awakened call!

The author

Decidation

I would like to dedicate this novel to my number one Fan -you know who you are- in appreciation for all her admiration and enthusiastic reader.

This fictional story was written while life was happening.

For a couple of years my life crossed with several beautiful beings and the story evolved to include them in it.

Life is composed of encounters that make the game of life become more enjoyable.

All of them have awakened my full creativity, and made recovered memories of a long past.

They become part of my Horizon Of Freedom.

Thank you for sharing your journey with me.

I will always remember your immense grandiosity as I grow in experience because of each one of you.

We will meet again on the STARS as a brotherhood

Chapter I - Time to Hidden

The big invasion just started to happen.

The Psycos take over the galactic kingdom.

Fer, walking for mountains hidden paths looking to organize his thoughts .

What just happened on this Macabe morning was totally irreal.

The Democratic Confederacy disappeared.

It is time to hide as on the sky patrol spaceships continue to eliminate anyone who doesn't follow the reclusion.

A suspicious movement calls the attention to Fer.

Pulling the lightsaber, getting in a defensive position.

The same way as a samurai will hold a weapon.

The sound emanating from the weapon makes a little boy come out.

Sir, don't kill us - says the boy.

A group of Elite cadets from the dead Macab Elite Confederation comes out.

Fer is totally astonished.

Nobody can ever know that they escaped.

Time to find a place to hide.

Chapter II - The Search

Up standing at one side of the room, Fer is putting all his spiritual perception in full alertness.

A tremendous amount of energy is flowing from him.

Suddenly, he "awakes".

Perceived a strong energy coming from the other side of the room.

Step out to look better.

"A young woman with light blue eyes" - Think Fer.

She looks in his direction like it is observed.

"Yes, she radiates that clear energy". Fer was no doubt that have spotted one of the Elite Force team.

Fer approach to put a communication line there.

And try to understand how "awake" she is.

As a magic moment the time stops, they start to talk in a physical way.

But both beings are totally in a spiritual universe "playing" like 2 kids.

Their eyes fixed like looking inside the souls of each other.

Fer, go away but can't hide his big happiness.

"Finding the number 3 of the 26 special beings " - Thinks Fer.

Each of the 26 coming from the 26 stars that compose the Galactic Confederation.

At that time it was part of a spiritual movement that 26 special beings have borne to take the galaxy to an up level of consciousness.

Each one with a very particular power, together complemented each other capable of extraordinary abilities.

"I had the privilege of living with this amazing group."

"I became the number 27",

Chapter III - Creating The Future

For a couple of days, Fer and the 26 cadets are walking on these unexplored mountains.

The two Sois align at this time of the year indicates the end of another era.

Crossing the purple sky two brontosaurus with big wings flying clumsily.

The kids pick up some edible roots while playing like innocent children.

Fer knows the importance of finding a place to put these kids in safety.

The rare sound of a cascade calls attention to all.

A group of three go to explore looking for another place to pass the darkness of the day.

Fer, testing the waters to find out if cleaning enough to be useful.

One of the exploring group girls made gestures calling our attention to walk over there.

Behind the cascade is an old hand made entrance.

The decision was to walk over and find a spot for rest.

The luminous lights emanated from some viscous slung allowing us to continue our journey through the enormous cave mountain.

Some purple lights are visible showing an exit.

The vision is impressive.

A microclimate has allowed to grow a giant forest with a large river and fields of beautiful blue flowers.

"Let's rest here.
Tomorrow we will explore it". Said Fer.

A new day arrived.

Pulling a strong cable prepared the descent that one by one made to the field below us.

We found our new home.

The place to create a future away from the madness of Macabe new order.

"I need to preserve and train the only chance this galaxy has.

They are the only hope".

Chapter IV - Time Secrets

On the Prison Planet, Fer continues his journey to find the Elite Team.

He can't lose sight of the 3 already found, especially because they are still in the process of coming out of the Matrix.

Walking on the clear night he looks to the sky.

"Right there, the star that brings light to Macabe ". His attention is fixed on the place where the planet can be found.

Fer lived for more than 35 million years in that area.

Implanted life after life was part of the engineering group of the Galactic Elite.

After being captured, he never got his freedom back.

Living a fake life programmed in the Matrix.

Around 3,000 years ago he got the opportunity to be pulled off.

Since then, he has fought for the freedom of others.

With all the memories back, recovery of all knowledge on the scientific field, engineering. Even the suppressive plans.

But more importantly, recover the secret of the universe.

Fer by helping the 26 Elite Team had got back the powers taught by then.

"I was only there to keep the group together ".

"I saw the power that each one can generate".

Probably the most amazing is the ability to pick up bodies without being noticed by the Prison guards.

"I never got back to the implant station ".

And that is the basic reason I'm so aware with my full power intact.

Fer, coming out of his thoughts, notices the most recent cadet approaching.

They start to talk in a very flowing manner.

It's amazing the amount of positive energy they generate when together.

It is very clear that their connection is very strong, really more strong than they can think.

The future will reveal it.

Fer says goodbye to Jo, but true of fact he will wish never to have to do it.

"We can be talking all day and all night .

It's the best feeling I have had for a long time".

Her power is to emanate harmony, the power to dissolve any energy turbulence.

Chapter V - A Place To Live

We have built our news houses on the high trees creating a triangular space.

The amount of animals and plants unknown to us is astounding.

Still learning and categories the dangers and friendly ones.

Creating a safe place where it can't be reached easily was the best solution.

Many moons have passed and not a single spaceship was detected.

However, we keep an observation post in case of any threat.

My role is to keep the discipline.

"Big beings in baby bodies".

All the time trying to make something funny using their powers on others.

From what I read from big books in the Galactic library, each of these illumines was born with a unique ability.

But the big power is the combination of all.

It took a long period of time with several thousand missions to find through the galaxy all of them.

My big challenge is to make them work as a team.

For me a pilot, an engineer trying to understand what for me was only a legend is something that I never thought possible.

But the more I spent the time with them the more I believe that there's a spiritual force involved with it.

All of them try to teach me some of their spiritual wisdom.

One of the first I started to get slightly controlled was jumping between the lapses of time.

Appear and disappear using this method to go to these places where there is no time.

A new day has just arrived to is ending

Everyone prepares to go back home.

Suddenly, a strike sounds.

Looking like an asteroid crossing the surface of the gravitation field of the planet.

Fer, an experienced pilot, perceives that it is not an asteroid.

It's a single spaceship, involved in a fireball crashing not far for them.

Fer gets his arm hairs rising, the body strangely trembling.

Too late to go to the rescue.

"Tomorrow first light".

Chapter VI - The Rescue

The first light of the day and Fer is ready to depart.

This rescue mission can be dangerous but Jo persuades me to take her.

Using my wrist geo location introduced the best possible way to get that crash place.

Walking down directions to the river below us.

The dangerous terrain and plants are a bit challenging.

"Things are pretty much easy". Thinks Fer.

For a moment, I look back and perceive that Jo using her power creates a sense of calmness.

By touching on the things where she passes.

I look at her in a thankful expression.

She smiles at me the innocent way that only a big being could do.

At that moment I perceive that she is there only to protect me.

I look back to the way in front of us with more determination and confidence.

My universe became so peaceful with the certainty that there will be a future.

Finally we arrived at the river.

Big animals that I never imagined could exist are eating on the bottom from the river.

Jo enters on the river water and one this creature puts her head down and raises her.

Sitting on the back of the animal invited me to join her.

I feel so blessed to be sharing life with her and the others.

Arriving at the other side of the river Jo touched the head of the creature like thanks for the help.

I don't know what to tell her, a tear of joy and happiness insisted on rolling out of my eyes.

A knowing sound in the sky makes me hide and touch Jo with my hand so she follows me.

A search flying device crosses the sky, looking for the same as we.

Not a good sign.

We need to move fast to reach the crashing landing area before anyone else.

Climbing this mountain in front of us will make it possible to see the place I marked on my wrist device.

With prudent caution I look over the edge of the mountain.

It's visible the destruction created by the forceful crash.

We started to run down very fast.

Time is crucial.

That spying device had seen this too.

A search team will be here in no time.

The spaceship is badly damaged but the protective capsule is intact not so far away.

I try to open it up, but the exterior mechanism is damaged.

Using my laser sword cut the protection panel and pulled the cable bypassing the open mechanism.

The round cover slides.

A uniform woman.

Fer turns her face.

"Eve !?"

Chapter VII - Changing Plans

Fer continues his journey of searching.

Until now one from Germane, another from Russian and Hungary.

For some reason they are spread across the world.

"I need to get some help with this ". Thinking Fer.

Walking up the street , he gets a thought of Eve.

Raised his eyes and there she was.

"Hi Fer," said her.

"What are you doing here?" Ask Fer.

"I was driving and suddenly found myself coming here ".

For a long time they didn't see each other.

"I was missing a lot of our talking times". Said Eve.

Fer is emanating all his admiration of the being that is Eve.

His eternal soulmate that for some reason of the destiny still doesn't recognise him as such.

Fer can't hold himself and push her body against him.

"It is so good to see you ". Tell Fer near her ear.

Both decided to go for dinner at the Hotel where Fer kissed her for the first time.

Eve is again alone, having left John some time ago.

Beautiful as ever, Fer can't take his eyes away from her.

Both involve a warm talking and Fer can't resist to take her hand over the table.

She looks at him, trying to resist but at the same time recovering the wonderful memories of both, leaves her hand so Fer can play with.

For a couple of hours Fer was relaxing surrounded by the joy of his soulmate.

Night goes high.

Fer tried his luck.
"Can I sleep with you tonight?" While walking out.

Eve turns her head and kisses him...on the face.

A couple of days passed and Fer decided to follow his theory.

Take a train to Paris, looking in France for one of the 26.

He knows the time is crucial.

Something is about to happen and Fer perceives that can't be a good thing.

More and more the prison guards are closing in to find him.

He needs to use all the abilities to appear and disappear without being noticed.

But his strong energy is not easy to hide.

Moving will be the best way.

While Fer thinks on this the train arrives at his destination.

Looking through the window, see one, then another suspicious man in a long coat.

"They are here ". Think Fer.

With determination, step out of the train.

Using the power of disguise passes very close to them without being noticed.

Fer, retains all his energy to not be detected.

Passing through, Fer turns his head to make sure that haven't been seen.

"Wow, very close".

"Time to turn this search more seriously

Chapter VIII - The Decision

Eve coming out of the unconscious caused by the strong impact.

Fer tries to take her out of the protective cage.

"What are you doing here?" Ask Fer.

"Looking for a way to escape from the destruction of my planet ". Eve replied.

Fer looks better to her.

"Aren't you the Ambassador from the Blue Planet?"

"Yes."

"We have been invaded by these psyc creatures. Nothing is more like than before ".

The conversation is interrupted by spaceship sounds approximation.

"Your spaceship was located, they expect to find someone here".

Fer, in a fast thinking.

"I need you to go with Jo".

"I go create a distraction with a fake path".

Fer picks up the hand of Jo.

"Take good care of her ".

Fer observes both leaving with relief.

Meanwhile starts to make an evident impression on the surface to distract attention.

Walking very fast through the forest, I try to think of the best way to escape.

Time passes and Fer is looking to make sure they will follow him.

Jo and Eve finally arrive at campus where all the other kids are waiting.

All of them are very excited to see someone new.

Eve feels overwhelmed with all this reality.

However, her thoughts are if Fer makes it or not.

Jo perceives it.

Putting her hand on Eve's back.

"He knows what is doing.

You will go find him again ".

Fer, find the cable left to access the cavern.

Climbing and pulling the cable to prevent anyone finding it.

Now, feeling safe, decide to rest and plan his next move.

"I need to find others that have not been affected by this incident".

Having prepared some rations, I walked to the town as my final destination.

The Search Mission

After taking his spaceship from the deepest part of a Tibetan lake, Fer began to frequently travel to planets where he had lived before.

The battle between spiritual beings and psycho beings began a long time ago.

The balance is very fragile, and Fer is on a mission to find the 26 spiritual beings that will help restore this sector of the Galaxy to its original, pure state.

Chapter XI - A Magic Moment

Another normal day in Fer's Earth routine.

More than twelve months had passed since Fer was betrayed by the one he thought he could grow old with.

It had been a very intense passion—Fer, as usual, gave himself completely.

But she decided to break up and disappear.

For a long time, Fer suffered from the weight of such intense feelings until he decided to abandon everything and dedicate his life to the service of others.

Fer closed his heart to any woman, to any form of love.

Now, he lives only to help others.

However, when the day comes to an end, Fer feels alone—an introvert burdened by a failed love life.

He opens the door, intending to complete another daily task.

A strange wave of energy hits him—something familiar.

A distant memory rises within him, like a fire rekindled in his heart.

Fer looks around.

"Where is this emotion coming from?"

In his line of sight, a beautiful woman locks eyes with him.

"Why is she waving at me?"

Fer can't resist. His body moves toward her, as if pulled by a tractor beam.

She stands up as he approaches.

A voluptuous, beautiful figure. Of 40 Earth years. A joyful expression. Green eyes that take his breath away.

—"What's your name?" he asks, unable to look away.

"Exactly the same color as mine," Fer thinks.

The sound of her voice is like birdsong.

—"My name is Moni."

Suddenly, words become meaningless. Their communication shifts to a spiritual level.

Fer needs to go, but he's unable to move away from that feeling.

"This woman brings memories from long ago."

He feels a wave of love and admiration—something only one soul across all his lifetimes has ever stirred in him.

Moni knows exactly what she wants.

"I want to make love to him."

Many months earlier, she had seen Fer in that very place. She hadn't forgotten him since.

"He is mine. I have to have him, no matter what."

She, like Fer, has endured two failed marriages.

To her, men are only for temporary company—no more attachments. Too painful.

Time seems to stop.

They find themselves in a parallel universe.

Fer eventually walks away from Moni, but he knows his life changed forever in that moment.

"She is the real love I left behind thirty-three lives ago, in the Tibetan plateau? No one else has this kind of light."

"I've found my soulmate again?"

Fer had already, long ago, felt a similar wavelength.

But this one was different—it felt like he had found the other half of himself.

"But how much does she remember about us?"

Chapter X - The Beginning

The day faded once more, and Fer returned to his small space to lay his body to rest.

A long day—full of emotions and memories.

As Fer's body rests, his mind drifts into distant memories.

"The strong magnetic field created by two giant planets gave birth to life forms.

Twenty-six new beings emerged.

Was it the magnetic field—or a Supreme Being—that brought forth this creation?"

Fer tries to visualize the memory.

What mattered most was that a powerful phenomenon caused each of the 26 beings to split into two halves.

Each half looked in a different direction, searching for a way to enjoy the pleasure of being free.

However, though they moved in opposite directions, they only made sense when they were together.

Suddenly, Fer comes to a realization.

"That's what I felt with this woman.

That's what I've been missing and searching for all this time.

"My other half."

"She is as powerful as I am."

And suddenly, everything made sense.

With each passing day, Fer finds himself constantly looking for Moni's presence.

No matter how difficult the day may be, everything fades away the moment he meets her gaze.

His heart starts to race like a wild horse.

Moni smiles at him, and he smiles back—like two teenagers in love.

Finally, they decide to find a quiet place to talk.

Fer feels he can no longer live without her.

Moni, too, cannot control the powerful feelings she has for him.

Alone at last, they hold each other tightly.

And the magic happens again.

Moni reveals her deep love for Fer.

Fer tells her it's impossible to resist her beauty.

At that moment, the world's clock stops.

Fer decides to share a memory he carries deep within him—a memory of his Soulmate.

Moni listens, and tears of joy begin to roll down her face.

Fer receives his confirmation.

Moni remembers that day on the Tibetan plateau, when Fer, as a samurai, died in her arms.

And the promise he made:

> "I will find you, my love—no matter how many lifetimes."

Now, they are together again.

Two halves, reunited as one.

Honor. Respect. Integrity— the three sacred principles of a Samurai and the True One.

Both realized that they could make sense together.

Not as a married couple in this lifetime, but as the two powerful beings they truly were.

"I'm here to help you achieve your goals," Fer said gently.

Tears of joy welled up on her face.

"Now I understand these strong feelings… You're my savior."

"Yes, Moni," Fer replied softly.

"Come with me. Let's join our strengths and create a better future—for us and for this planet."

"And how do you know?" she asked, her voice trembling.

"In the next lifetime... Can we recreate this love, this feeling, as a couple again?"

Chapter XI - A Warrior Of Other Times

One more time, Fer approached the edge of the Galaxy, where a small solar system was located: the Prison Planet.

Passing very close to the Yellow Star, he reached the third planet.

The planet's rudimentary radars couldn't detect the spacecraft—not even the proton traces from its engine.

Fer decided to land in the English countryside, in a location he knew well.

Dressing properly to blend in with the natives, Fer directed his spaceship to the bottom of a lake where no one would be able to find it.

It was a beautiful day. Using one of the local modes of transportation, Fer headed toward the sea—

The place that filled him with joy and the best memories of past lifetimes.

His attention was caught by a beautiful woman taking selfies near the water.

She had completed 36 revolutions around the Sun, but looked as if she were no older than 26.

Fer smiled at the way she was enjoying herself.

As he walked, he was drawn toward a small spot where some lovely music was playing.

He looked—and saw the same woman had stopped there too.

Fer was hypnotized by her big, blue eyes.

"Are you on vacation like me?" Fer asked.

She answered.

Her voice stirred something deep inside Fer. He wanted to know this beautiful woman.

"Can I invite you for a coffee?" Fer tried not to sound strange.

She smiled and said, "Yes."

"I'm Fer. And you?"

"Mer."

Their conversation flowed easily. It was light, natural, and enjoyable.

For a brief moment, Fer was pulled back inside his own mind.

"She has all the characteristics of the amazing spiritual beings I'm looking for," he thought.

Her spiritual energy… the vivid life in her blue eyes…

Suddenly, Fer remembered the last time their lives had crossed:

The Byzantine Empire, where modern-day Turkey is now.

Mer had been the wife of a powerful warrior.

By the 12th century, the Sultanate of Rum controlled much of central Anatolia, standing as a major Turkish Muslim power in the region.

After her husband was killed in an ambush, Mer took up his swords and fought for the freedom of her people.

She became a legend.

Fer had been there. People said she had defeated an entire army of 100 men—alone.

Turkey exists today in part due to her determination and courage.

Fer snapped back to the present, returning mentally to the chair in front of Mer.

"I need to go," she said.

Fer had hoped to spend the whole day with her, but didn't want to impose his presence .

"Can I have your contact?" he asked.

They said goodbye.

Fer knew they would meet again.

She was one of the 26 extraordinary beings—each with a unique power.

Her power was STRENGTH.

The ability to defeat any opponent.

She was number 7 of those Fer had found so far.

The search continue

CHAPTER XII - The Sweet Italian

Suddenly, Fer receives a notification on his device.

"How are you?"

He looks at the screen and her face brings memories.

"It's me, Angy. We met last year."

The memory hit Fer.

"How is it possible, I forgot her? That fragile Italian woman with big blue eyes."

Fer smiles

"Looks like my search motion starts to attract the other 26 beings.

Angy, the number 8.

Hope, from Spain the number 9."

One after the other, Fer started to attract attention from all of them around the world.

Everything was about to change.

CHAPTER XIII - The Way Out

Six months passed by.

Fer had found the 26 being.

From all ages of Earth time.

Each one at different levels of awareness and understanding.

But miraculously when brought together like they recognise each other.

The battle for freedom or darkness is in balance.

The attacks from the psycho each time are more and more strong.

The freedom path is in risk of being closed forever.

Fer remember some valuable words... "the only way to stop this dwelling spiral to darkness is to undo the incident ".

For a long period of time this kept on Fer's head.

"Can this be possible to accomplish?"

He looks at the group and all his good memories coming to him.

Turning to the group to ask for their attention.

Eve makes them calm down and listen.

"I have an idea...that is very dangerous and needs to be executed very quickly.

We need transportation to fly to Marcab."

"What???" Says Eve.

"The only way to undo all these things will be back to the same place where the incident occurred crossing it at the exact location and time as it happened". Continues Fer.

"We need to go all together to the Yellow River in Tibet.

Bring my spaceship from the bottom of the lake and fly away .

Let's go, I will explain all in our way ".

In small groups they start to travel abroad by train.

Destination: Japan, the Tibet plateau.

CHAPTER XIV - Running Against Time

For a couple of days they walked through the mountains that will bring them to the place that Fer described.

Fer and Eve just came to the top of an elevation.
Stopped and smiled at each other.

Her memories come back.

There was the place where they lived when Fer was a samurai and recognised Eve as his soulmate.

Eve gave him her hand and an inevitable kiss.

"We are near.
The lake is just over the other side".

While walking on other times they land, traces of the construction and vegetable fields are still recognised.

Fer remembers the exact place where he left his body in the arms of his soulmate.

Fer strongly holds Eve's hand.

She looks at him as confirmation that she recalls it too.

The group is already on the other side looking at the enormous lake that the Yellow River fills.

Fer starts to look inside for his memories of more than 3000 years ago.

Point to a pile of rocks.

From there you can see the lake.

"It's right here". Says he.

Moving all the debris a small entrance into the rock becomes visible.

Fer introduced his hand and recovered a small device.

Everyone is watching him.

"This is the dangerous part.

The moment I activate it a signal will be sent and Marcab controls will be alerted.

A patrol officer will be dispatched to check.

Remember, I am still the most wanted man on the Galaxy".

Everyone laughs.

Fer put his finger over and in no time big bubbles were forming on the lake water.

The old spaceship is brought to land.

Jo says "it's so small, how can we fit all inside?"

"This is the other part that I haven't told.

I need to go alone to one of the Marcab moons and steal a cargo spaceship and back."

"You say it as something easy.

Have you done this before?"

Eve looks very apprehensive.

"Yes and this is the only chance and now there is no more way back." Reply.

Inside the small space, with the uniform on. Look at the control panel that at his time was activated by voice.

"I don't think my voice now will be recognised." Thinks Fer.

Close his eyes and in a flash back gets the idea how to turn off the sound activation and put his hands on the keyboard.

Everyone gives space while the spaceship starts to move upward.

Marcab's traffic control officer is very confused with the light on his screen.

Call a senior officer as he doesn't understand what is that movement on that far planet.

He sees that a vehicle crosses light speed and has no authorized flight direct to the planet.

Immediately gives the alert to the outside defenses.

CHAPTER XV - The No Return Flight

Fer thinks to himself, "hope that nothing has changed in this last 3000 years".

Making a detour behind the big Moon of Marcab, Fer tries to avoid the planet's defenses.

Defensive responses try to contact the spaceship without success.

"Number and rank?
You are violating defensive protocols.
No authorisation to approach the planet".

Meantime, the light on the big control screen disappeared.

Fer, using the covering of the colossal Moon, flies now to the second Moon.

An old mine from where is extracted de mineral to build the spaceship structure.

Knowing very well the place, for the many lifetimes before, Fer descends on the official platform.

The security is minimal.

Fer, in his uniform and cape feels very comfortable.

The guard behind the curve window sees him.

Fer, make a salute gesture to the guard.

While in a decisive walk make his entrance on the big hangar where several space cargo waiting for his turn to load.

The rear ramp is open and Fer walks inside one of it

"Side seats", observe.

Seats at the controls and instantly comes to him with the knowledge to put the big "bird" a couple centimeters above the floor.

Take a deep breath.

"So far so good".

Exiting from the hangar, the guard didn't put too much attention on it.

Fer started to think that need to find a route away from the planet but a common one that didn't attract attention.

A couple of cargo ships fly a commercial route to a neighboring planet.

Quickly fly to the back and align with them.

At a secure distance, introduced Earth coordinates.

Using a wormhole jump near Venus, making the approach using the Sunlight to not be seen.

Rudimentary Earth radar can't detect the structure defection of the spaceship.

Soon back to the same place from where he had departed.

The heavy ramps open and Fer comes out.

"Ready for a ride?" Smiles to the group like he has done something ordinary.

Everyone inside, Eve seating at Fer side.

Look at him. "What is the plan?"

Moving his shoulders according to his comment. "For the first time in my life I don't have a plan ".

"Only I know I need to take the 26 crossing incident and that will undo the catastrophe".

The moment they've crossed the Earth screen, Fer perceived an abnormal movement of fighters.

Decide to change route and find another wormhole near Saturn.

"What happens?" Ask Eve.

"Patrol spaceships are following my flight traces.

We need a different way."

Existing far away from the central planet that is Marcab, Fer knows the importance of acting quickly.

After having introduced the known coordinates, where millions of years ago life had changed on these galaxy sectors.

Fer and Eve cross the door where all the 26 are seated.

"This will be a no return flight.
We will put all the universe's faith into your hands."

Eve gave her hand to Fer.

"We don't care what may happen to us, just please save it."

Looking to Fer as talking for both.

The 26 give their hands to each other forming a circle.

An enormous amount of energy is generated.

The digital clock shows the remaining time…3…2…1.

CHAPTER XVI - Year Zero

"Wow.
The speed of this fight ship is vertiginous". Tell Fer to his colleagues by communicator installed in his fight helmet.

"Take it easy.
You don't want to crash on the first flight, correct?" His big friend continued the communication.

Fer laughs

"As that will be the first time..."

The well established fleet of crusaders and fighters are ready for action.

The entrance of a new species on the Galactic sector makes things become agitated.

In the Senators assembly the tension can be perceived.

The Blue Planet's Ambassador, Eve, asks permission to speak.

Her pod flight to the center with her advisers.

"In the name of the Blue Planet Democratic Republic and all our partners.

We decide not to recognise as beneficial for this Galaxy sector the entrance of this new espécie.

It's conclusive that WE don't need or wish to use implants or drugs in these old civilisations.

We are spiritual beings, no bodies.

Our vote is NO."

An enormous noise invading the room.

Back to Macabe planet, Fer enjoys a couple of days as the War declaration was canceled.

Smiling as usual looks like nothing bad can happen to him.

His happiness and light approach to life are his best characteristics.

Crossing the door of the engineering class, stop to look through the transparent ceiling.

The purple light became visible.

Starting to walk when noticed a young light blue-eyed girl that comes in the opposite direction with her mother.

She passes by and a couple of steps turn her head and blink the right eye to Fer.

He feels that all the millions of years just happened a minute ago.

All his memories come back to him.

Jo, raising her little hand to him, as saying goodbye.

Fer, smile at her, while raising his hand too.

The good will prevail, as good are the souls of all beings.

The undo of that catastrophe will happen.

Keep admiring life as admiration will bring back life to is native state.

THE END

www.ingramcontent.com/pod-product-compliance
Lightning Source LLC
Chambersburg PA
CBHW071255070526
44583CB00017B/2480